CULTURE IN ACTION

Poetry

Elizabeth Raum

Raintree

Chicago, Illinois

www.heinemannraintree.com
Visit our website to find out more information about Heinemann-Raintree books.

To order:

☎ Phone 888-454-2279
🖥 Visit www.heinemannraintree.com to browse our catalog and order online.

Edited by Louise Galpine, Abby Colich, and Laura J. Hensley
Designed by Kimberly Miracle and Betsy Wernert
Original illustrations © Capstone Global Library Ltd.
Illustrated by kja-artists.com
Picture research by Mica Brancic and Kay Altwegg
Production by Alison Parsons
Originated by Dot Gradations Ltd.
Printed in China by Leo Paper Products Ltd

13 12 11 10 09
10 9 8 7 6 5 4 3 2 1

Library of Congress Cataloging-in-Publication Data
Raum, Elizabeth.
  Poetry / Elizabeth Raum.
    p. cm. -- (Culture in action)
  Includes bibliographical references and index.
  ISBN 978-1-4109-3404-8 -- ISBN 978-1-4109-3421-5 (pbk.)
  1. Poetry--Juvenile literature. I. Title.
  PN1031.R36 2009
  808.1--dc22
                          2009000418

Acknowledgments

The author and publishers are grateful to the following for permission to reproduce copyright material: ©Alamy p. **27** (UpperCut Images); ©Corbis pp. **6** (Bettmann), **8** (Bettmann), **9** (Cynthia Hart Designer), **10** (Star Ledger/Robert Sciarrino), **12** (Stapleton Collection), **15** (Bettmann), **16** (Blue Lantern Studio), **19** (The Gallery Collection), **20** (Lebrecht Music & Arts), **21** (Bettmann), **22 top** (Francis G. Mayer), **22 bottom** (Francis G. Mayer), **24** (epa/Adrian Bradshaw), **25** (Asian Art & Archaeology, Inc.); ©Getty Images pp. **4** (The Bridgeman Art Library), **5 bottom** (AFP/Odd Andersen), **17** (Hulton Archive), **18** (The Bridgeman Art Library), **26** (AFP), **29** (FilmMagic/Steve Mack); ©Mary Evans Picture Library pp. **13**, **14**; ©PA Photos pp. **5 top** (All Action.co.uk), **7** (Empics Entertainment).

Icon and banner images supplied by Shutterstock: © Alexander Lukin, © ornitopter, © Colorlife, and © David S. Rose.

Cover photograph of African man reading into microphone reproduced with permission of Photolibrary/ Blend Images/ Andersen Ross.

"TEN: NIL" by Celia Warren, reprinted with permission of the author; "Keep a Poem in Your Pocket" by Beatrice Schenk de Regniers, from *Something Special* by Beatrice Schenk de Regniers. Copyright © 1958, 1986 by Beatrice Schenk de Regniers. Used by permission of Marian Reiner.

We would like to thank Nancy Harris, Jackie Murphy, and Tristan Boyer Binns for their invaluable help in the preparation of this book.

Contents

Some words are printed in bold, **like this**. You can find out what they mean by looking in the glossary on page 30.

The Music of Poetry

You listen to poetry every day. Surprised? Don't be. Poetry is all around you. You probably hear it most often as song. The words of songs, called **lyrics**, are a kind of poetry. Most poems, including songs, are called **lyric poems**. They express the poet's feelings and personal experiences.

> " Poetry is the record of the best and happiest moments of the happiest and best minds."
>
> —English poet Percy Bysshe Shelley

A poem may make us feel happy or sad. It may remind us of other times and places. Well-written poems make us notice the world around us and think about the way we live.

The lyre

In ancient Greece, poets often played a stringed instrument called a lyre while **reciting** poetry (repeating it from memory). The word *lyric*, used to describe a kind of poetry, comes from the Greek word *lyre*. So does the word *lyrics*. This is used to describe the words to a song.

This painting shows the poet Homer singing and playing his lyre in ancient Greece.

This photo of the Beatles shows (clockwise from left) Paul McCartney, John Lennon, George Harrison, and Ringo Starr.

The Beatles

From 1958 to 1969, Paul McCartney and John Lennon of the Beatles wrote more than 200 songs together. The lyrics of their songs are poems. The Beatles had more number-one hits and sold more albums around the world than any other musical group.

What is poetry?

Poetry looks different from other kinds of writing. Poetry is written in lines rather than sentences. A line might have only one or two words, or it might stretch across the entire page. Lines are divided into **stanzas**, or groupings of two or more lines. Breaks in the Beatles' lyrics (see photo at right) divide a song into stanzas.

Hey Jude - don't make it bad,
take a sad song and make it better,
Remember to let her into your heart,
then you can start to make it better.

Hey Jude don't be afraid
You were made to go out and get her,
the minute you let her under your skin
Then you'll begin to make it better.

And any time you feel the pain
hey Jude refrain don't carry the world upon
                                    your shoulders

For well you know that's it, a fool who plays it cool
by making his (life) (world) a little colder.

Hey Jude don't let me down.
She had found you now make it better
Remember to let her into your heart,
then you can start to make it better.
So let it out and let it in, hey Jude begin
    you waiting for someone to perform with
+ don't you know that it's just you

Paul McCartney and John Lennon, of the Beatles, wrote the song "Hey Jude." Notice how this original copy of the lyrics is set up like a poem.

5

The Poet's Tools

Words are the building blocks of poetry. Poets choose words that create pictures in our minds. They use words and phrases that remind us of how things sound, smell, taste, or feel. Words that appeal to our senses make the poem more meaningful.

Rhyme

The repetition of sounds at the end of words or lines is called a **rhyme**. Rhyme sometimes occurs within lines, too. Notice how the lines rhyme in this poem by Emily Dickinson:

> A bird came down the walk:
> He did not know I saw;
> He bit an angle-worm in halves
> And ate the fellow, raw.

In this poem, lines two and four rhyme. Poets use many different rhyming patterns, or **rhyme schemes**.

Emily Dickinson lived from 1830 until 1886.

"If I feel physically as if the top of my head were taken off, I know that is poetry."
—U.S. poet Emily Dickinson

Free verse

Not all poems rhyme. Poems that do not rhyme are called **free verse**.

This poem created by the Yuma people, who lived in the southwestern United States, is an example of free verse:

> ## "Water Bug"
> The water bug
> is drawing the shadows of evening
> Toward him across the water.

Rhythm

The beat created by a poem's words is its **rhythm**. When we read, we **stress** some **syllables** (units of sound) more than others. This creates a rhythm like the beat in music. For example, in the first line of Dickinson's poem on page 6, we stress the words *bird*, *down*, and *walk*. In the second line, we stress *did*, *know*, and *saw*. Read the poem aloud. Can you hear the rhythm?

Rap is a kind of poetry that people **recite** to a strong drumbeat. This photo shows the rapper Lupe Fiasco.

Playing with sound

Poets choose words for their sound as well as for their meaning. Sometimes poets use **alliteration**, the repetition of beginning letters and sounds. Tongue twisters use alliteration. Most poets repeat a sound only once or twice.

Assonance is the repetition of vowel sounds within words that are used close to each other. The words *make* and *late* used in a sentence or poem are an example of assonance. They do not rhyme, but they both have the same long *a* sound.

Peter Piper pick'd a Peck of Pickled
  Peppers:
Did Peter Piper pick a Peck of Pickled
  Peppers?
If Peter Piper pick'd a peck of Pickled
  Peppers,
Where's the Peck of Pickled Peppers
  Peter Piper pick'd ?

Can you say this tongue twister without tripping over the *P*s?

The English poet Lewis Carroll played with sound in a **nonsense poem** called "Jabberwocky." Read this **stanza** out loud. Most of the words are made up. Do they make sense? Notice Carroll's use of alliteration and assonance. Words that sound like the thing they describe are called **onomatopoeia**. When you say a duck makes a "quack" sound, you are using onomatopoeia.

"Jabberwocky" by Lewis Carroll

'Twas brillig, and the slithy toves
Did **g**yre and **g**imble in the wabe: [Alliteration in **g** sound]
All mimsy were the bor**og**oves,
And the m**o**me raths outgrabe.   [Assonance in **o** sound]

How to read poetry aloud

Poetry is fun to read aloud. But before you read for others, do the following:

- Learn how to pronounce any unfamiliar words. Check a dictionary or ask someone if you need help.

- Try to understand the poem's meaning so that you can express it to others.

- Pay attention to punctuation. If there is a period, stop. If there is a comma, pause. If there is no punctuation, continue reading. Read the poem in a way that makes sense.

- Read with feeling. Think about how fast or slowly you should read the poem. How should your voice sound? Happy? Excited? Sad? Should the poem be read loudly or quietly? Practice until you can read smoothly and with feeling.

Greeting cards like this 1912 Valentine often include short poems.

Love's fond Greeting

My heart, as tender as can be,
  Enfolds the fondest love for thee.
Pray, let my thoughts encompass thine,
  And take me for thy Valentine.

Choral reading

When two or more people read a poem together, it is called a choral reading. Choral reading is a fun way to share poems. Preparing a choral reading is like putting on a play without using costumes or props. You do not even have to memorize your lines.

You may hold a copy of the poem you are reading, but keep books or papers away from your face. You can also use your hands and face to help show a poem's meaning, as this girl is doing.

Steps to follow:

1. Choose a friend or two to read with you.

2. Select poems to read aloud. (See page 31 for suggestions, or try "Tip-a-Toe," below.)

3. Assign different lines to different readers, or read the poem together.

4. Give everyone a copy of the poem. Read your parts aloud. Look back at page 9 for some tips on how to read a poem aloud.

5. Stand together or sit on stools at the front of the room. Make sure someone announces the title of the poem and the poet before reading each poem.

"Tip-a-Toe" by Kate Greenaway

Tip-a-Toe,
See them go;
One, two, three—
Chloe, Prue, and me;
Up and down,
To the town.
A Lord was there,
And the Lady fair.
And what did they sing?
Oh, "Ring-a-ding-ding;"
And the Black Crow flew off
With the Lady's Ring.

Poems That Tell Stories

No one knows exactly when or where poetry began. The first poems were probably songs or **chants**. A chant is a phrase repeated in **rhythm** (regular beats). Many ancient poems honored gods and heroes.

An **epic** poem describes the adventures of a hero. Epics have been written throughout the world. *Gilgamesh* is one of the earliest epic poems. It tells the story of Gilgamesh, a king from ancient Mesopotamia, in Asia. It was created about 4,000 years ago.

The blind poet Homer told stories of Greek heroes. Odysseus is the hero of Homer's epic poem *The Odyssey*. His epic poem *The Iliad* is about the Greek warrior Achilles. High school and college students study these poems, which were written nearly 3,000 years ago.

This painting is based on Homer's epic poem *The Odyssey*. It shows Odysseus standing on his ship.

Beowulf was written about 1,300 years ago in England. It tells the story of a Swedish hero named Beowolf. About 1,000 years ago, *The Song of Roland* was written in France about a Frenchman named Roland. Viking sagas are from Scandinavia. They are another kind of epic poem.

Canterbury Tales

One of the most famous epics in English is the *Canterbury Tales* by Geoffrey Chaucer. This long poem entertained early listeners. It still does. The *Canterbury Tales* also tells us much about how people used to live.

The poem tells the story of a traveler on a journey to Canterbury, a town in England, in the 1300s. While staying at an inn, he meets 29 other people taking the same journey. The innkeeper suggests that each traveler tell a tale. The winner will earn a free dinner at the inn. The travelers include a nun, a knight, and a merchant.

English poet Geoffrey Chaucer lived from about 1340 to 1400.

Narrative poems

Poems that tell a story or describe a special event are called **narrative poems** or dramatic poems. These poems usually have several **stanzas**, but they are not as long as epics.

In the 1800s and 1900s, children would learn narrative poems by heart and **recite** them for school and community events. Narrative poems use **rhyme**, rhythm, and lively description to entertain listeners.

> "The idea is to write so that people hear it and it slides through the brain and goes straight to the heart."
>
> —U.S. poet Maya Angelou

"Paul Revere's Ride" by Henry Wadsworth Longfellow

One of the most famous U.S. narrative poems is Henry Wadsworth Longfellow's "Paul Revere's Ride," about the Revolutionary War hero. Notice how Longfellow addresses his poem directly to his listeners.

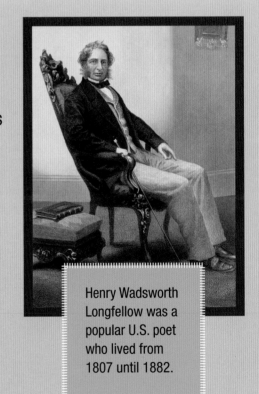

Listen, my children, and you shall hear
Of the midnight ride of Paul Revere,
On the eighteenth of April, in Seventy-Five;
Hardly a man is now alive
Who remembers that famous day and year.

Henry Wadsworth Longfellow was a popular U.S. poet who lived from 1807 until 1882.

Ballads

Story poems with short stanzas are called **ballads**. Ballads began to appear in Europe between 1,000 and 1,500 years ago. Wandering storytellers traveled from town to town singing ballads.

Many of today's popular songs are ballads. A famous ballad from the 1800s was called "The Daring Young Man on the Flying Trapeze." The chorus begins:

He flies through the air with the greatest of ease
This daring young man on the flying trapeze.

Longfellow used an event in U.S. history, the ride of Paul Revere, as the subject of a narrative poem.

Playing with Poetry

Parents around the world sing lullabies to their children and tell them nursery **rhymes**. These are the first poems that most children hear. On the playground, children often **chant** jump-rope rhymes and laugh over riddles, tongue twisters, and other silly poems. Poetry is fun. Poets often write poems to amuse children and to help us see the world in new ways.

Old Mother Goose, when
She wanted to wander,
Would ride through the air
On a very fine gander.

Some nursery rhymes, such as "Mother Goose," are hundreds of years old.

"TEN: NIL" by Celia Warren

The phantom fans are chanting.
There's a cheer in my ear as I score.
I've done it again: ten goals to me
And nil to the garage door!

" Poetry is what makes me laugh or cry or yawn, what makes my toenails twinkle."
—Welsh poet Dylan Thomas

Limericks

In the 1800s, English poet Edward Lear entertained children and adults with **nonsense poems** called **limericks**. A limerick is a funny poem that has five lines. Lines 1, 2, and 5 rhyme and are longer (7 to 10 **syllables**). Lines 3 and 4 rhyme and are shorter (5 to 7 syllables). Lear's nonsense poems sold well. Today, many experts consider Lear a genius for writing his clever poems.

Edward Lear lived from 1812 to 1888. This drawing is from 1840.

An Edward Lear limerick

There was a Young Lady whose bonnet
Came untied when the birds sate upon it;
But she said, "I don't care!
All the birds in the air
Are welcome to sit on my bonnet!"

Children's poet laureates

Many countries honor children's poets by naming someone as a children's poet **laureate**. This award honors the contributions the poet has made to children's poetry. He or she visits schools and presents programs on television and radio that encourage children to enjoy poetry.

Write and illustrate your own limerick

For this activity, you will write and illustrate your own limerick.

Steps to follow:

1. Fold a piece of paper in half. On one half you will write a limerick. On the other you will create a fun drawing based on the limerick.

2. Read the limerick on page 17 out loud. Listen for the **rhythm** and **rhyme scheme**.

3. Write your own limerick. Remember that lines 1, 2, and 5 will be 7 to 10 syllables long. The last word of each of these lines will rhyme. Lines 3 and 4 are 5 to 7 syllables long and rhyme with each other.

4. Use the other half of the page to create a silly and fun drawing based on your limerick.

5. Share your limerick so that others can enjoy your work.

Lear drew this picture of himself as an old man with his cat Foss. He often illustrated his limericks.

The boy on the left is reading the first two lines of his limerick to his friends. The limerick begins:

There was a wild zebra named Bill
Who fell from the top of a hill.

The Language of Poetry

Writing a poem is like doing a puzzle. The words must fit together to create something completely new. William Shakespeare chose words carefully when he wrote his poems. Even though Shakespeare wrote more than 400 years ago, people still enjoy his writing.

Read the poem below. Notice how Shakespeare combines words in new ways. For example, he does not simply say "newt." He makes it more exact— "eye of newt."

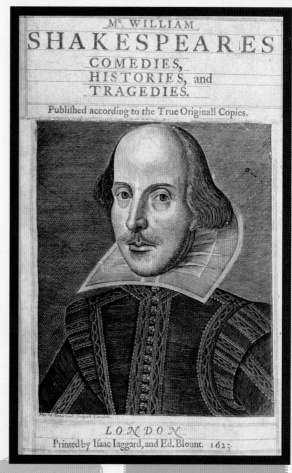

Mr. WILLIAM

SHAKESPEARES

COMEDIES,
HISTORIES, and
TRAGEDIES.

Published according to the True Originall Copies.

LONDON

Printed by Isaac Iaggard, and Ed. Blount. 1623.

William Shakespeare (1564–1616) was one of England's most famous poets.

From "The Witches' Song," in Shakespeare's play *Macbeth*

Eye of newt, and toe of frog,
Wool of bat, and tongue of dog,
Adder's fork, and blink-worm's sting,
Lizard's leg, and howler's wing,
For a charm of powerful trouble,
Like a hell-broth boil and bubble.
Double, double toil and trouble;
Fire burn and cauldron bubble.

Figurative language

Figurative language is speech or writing that departs from exact meaning to achieve a special effect. Three kinds of figurative language are **simile**, **metaphor**, and **personification**. Each of these tools can be used to compare unlike things. Figurative language creates a picture in our minds. It makes a poem easier to understand.

Simile

A simile is a comparison using the words *like* or *as*. Robert Louis Stevenson used simile when he wrote the first line of his poem "The Moon":

> The moon has a face like the clock in the hall.

Poet Edna St. Vincent Millay used simile in her poem "Sorrow":

> Sorrow like a ceaseless rain
> Beats upon my heart.

Poet William Wordsworth also used simile in his poem "Daffodils":

> I wandered lonely as a cloud
> That floats on high o'er vales and hills.

Robert Louis Stevenson was a Scottish poet and writer who lived from 1850 to 1894.

Metaphor

A metaphor is a direct comparison of two unlike things. It does not use *like* or *as*. Poet Rowena Bastin Bennett used metaphor when she wrote the following line in her poem "A Modern Dragon":

A train is a dragon that roars through the dark.

Notice that she did not use the comparing words *like* or *as*.

Personification

Giving human traits to animals, objects, or ideas is called personification. Poet Christina Rossetti used personification to bring the sea to life in her poem "By the Sea":

Why does the sea moan evermore?
Shut out from heaven it makes its moan,
It frets against the boundary shore.

In his poem "The Cloud," poet Percy Bysshe Shelley used personification to describe flowers:

I bring fresh showers for the thirsting flowers.

Christina Rossetti was an English poet who lived from 1830 to 1894.

Making meaning

Good poems make us think. Poets use strong words and figurative language to create pictures in our minds. Poets also use words to create a certain mood or feeling.

Some poems seem dark. Others are light and joyful. The sounds, **rhymes**, **rhythms**, and punctuation help to create both meaning and feeling.

When you read the poem below, think about how it makes you feel. What is its mood?

"Spring"
by William Blake

Sound the flute!
Now it's mute!
Birds delight
Day and night;
Nightingale
In the dale,
Lark in the sky,—
Merrily,
Merrily, merrily to
welcome in the year.

Like poets, artists also create moods or feelings in their work. Grant Reynard, the artist who painted these pictures of the sea, created two very different moods. How did the painter use light and color to create a different mood in each painting?

Write a song

For this exercise, you will create a poem of your own.

Steps to follow:

1. Listen to a favorite song with words. What is it about? Is it happy or sad?

2. Write down the first **stanza** of the song. Do the **lyrics** rhyme? Can you hear the rhythm? Circle the words that give you a strong picture or feeling.

3. Create your own lyrics. Write new words for this song. It might be about school, friends, family, or a favorite activity. Create a mood or feeling that fits with the music. Remember that rhythm is important. The lyrics must fit the music.

4. When you are done, sing your new song. Does it work? If not, change a word or two to make the words fit the music's beat. Share your song with friends.

Did you enjoy writing lyrics? Is it easy or difficult? Would you enjoy being a songwriter or poet?

World of Poetry

People all over the world write and enjoy poetry. Poetry written in other parts of the world may differ from the poems of North America and Europe. For example, ancient Hebrew songs and poems seldom used **rhyme**. They used repetition instead.

India's *Rig Veda* is an ancient collection of more than 1,000 **Hindu** poems. They are about nature, the seasons, and everyday life. These poems have **rhythm**, but they do not rhyme.

Poetry of Asia

Many Chinese poems have rhymes both within lines and at the end of lines. Some ancient poems in China had four Chinese **characters** (figures or marks used in writing) per line. Later, they would have either five or seven characters per line.

Modern Chinese poetry is usually written as **free verse**. Some Chinese poems are written in calligraphy. This fancy writing (see scroll in photo at right) combines poetry with art.

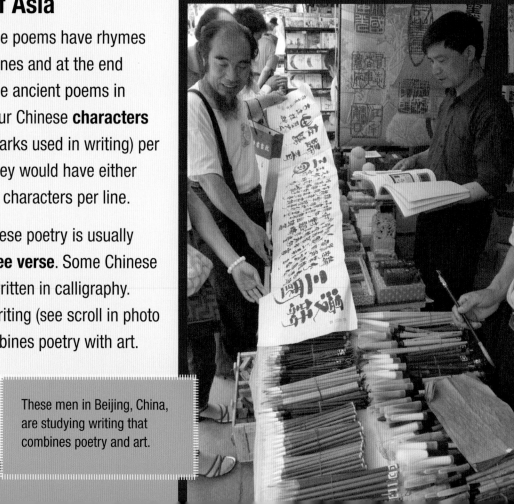

These men in Beijing, China, are studying writing that combines poetry and art.

Tanka is a type of Japanese poem that has five lines divided into two parts. The first part of a tanka is called the hokku, or "starting poem." It has 3 lines and 17 **syllables**. The last part has 2 lines of 14 syllables.

Many poets wrote just the hokku part of the tanka. These poems would later be called **haiku**. Haiku is popular throughout the world. Many children write haiku in school. Count the syllables in the two poems by Matsuo Bashō below.

Wrapping dumplings in
bamboo leaves, with one finger
she tidies her hair.

All day in gray rain
hollyhocks follow the sun's
invisible road.

Matsuo Bashō (1644–1694) was one of Japan's greatest poets.

Poems in other languages

Poets usually write poetry in their native language. For example, Japanese poets write in Japanese. Since not many people in the United States speak Japanese, we depend on translators to change the words into English.

However, changing the language changes the poem. Poets choose their words carefully. They choose words for meaning, sound, or rhythm. Translators try to keep the meaning and rhythm as close as possible to the original poem.

Poetry for everyone

People of all ages enjoy poetry. A short poem can capture a moment in time. A long poem can tell a story. Everyone brings his or her own ideas and experiences to poetry.

" Writing a poem is discovering."
—U.S. poet Robert Frost

Reading poetry can help us to see the world around us in new and different ways. Reading poetry can make us think about the way we live today, or it can give us a picture of the past.

This girl is reading poetry to children in India.

Writing poetry

Writing poetry is a way to share ideas. Anyone can write a poem. Writing poetry does not require permission or special equipment. All that is needed is a pen or a pencil, a piece of paper, and an idea or feeling. A poem can be short or long. It can rhyme, but it does not have to. It might be new words set to a favorite song. Go ahead—give poetry a try.

Writing poetry can be fun. It can also help you put words to your thoughts and feelings.

"Keep a Poem in Your Pocket"
by Beatrice Schenk de Regniers

Keep a poem in your pocket
and a picture in your head
and you'll never feel lonely
at night when you're in bed.

A Few Great Poets

Homer

Homer may have lived in ancient Greece. His exact birthplace and the dates of his birth and death are not known.

Occupation: **Epic** poet

Best known for *The Odyssey* and *The Iliad*

The ancient Greeks believed that Homer was a real historical person, but some experts question whether or not he really existed.

Geoffrey Chaucer (about 1345–1400)

Born: London, England

Occupation: Writer

Best known for **narrative poetry**, such as the *Canterbury Tales*

Chaucer is considered the first English poet.

William Shakespeare (1564–1616)

Born: Stratford-upon-Avon, England

Occupation: Playwright, poet

Best known for *Romeo and Juliet* and other plays written in poetic form. They are still performed today on stage and in film.

Shakespeare is often considered the greatest English writer of all time.

Matsuo Bashō (1644–1694)

Born: Japan

Occupation: Poet, travel writer

Best known for poems called **haiku**

Bashō traveled throughout Japan and wrote diaries about his journeys.

William Blake (1757–1827)

Born: London, England

Occupation: Poet, artist

Best known for **lyric poems**, such as those included in *Songs of Innocence*

Blake created the artwork for his books of poetry.

Henry Wadsworth Longfellow (1807–1882)

Born: Portland, Maine

Occupation: Writer, teacher

Best known for the narrative poems "Paul Revere's Ride," "The Song of Hiawatha," and "Evangeline"

Longfellow was one of the most popular poets of the 1800s.

Edward Lear (1812–1888)

Born: London, England

Occupation: Artist, poet, illustrator

Best known for his **nonsense poems**

Lear spent much of his life traveling throughout Europe.

Emily Dickinson (1830–1886)

Born: Amherst, Massachusetts

Occupation: Poet

Best known as one of the greatest U.S. writers of lyric poems

Dickinson wrote about 1,775 poems during her lifetime, but only 10 were published before her death.

Christina Rossetti (1830–1894)

Born: London, England

Occupation: Poet

Best known for a long poem called *Goblin Market*, religious poems, and poems written for children

Rossetti was part of a well-known creative family. Her father was a poet, and her brothers and sister were talented writers and artists.

Lewis Carroll (1832–1898)

(Carroll's real name was Charles Dodgson)

Born: Cheshire, England

Occupation: Mathematician, writer

Best known for novels and nonsense poems, such as *Alice in Wonderland* and *Through the Looking Glass*

Carroll wrote his novels especially for a girl named Alice.

Robert Louis Stevenson (1850–1894)

Born: Edinburgh, Scotland

Occupation: Writer, poet

Best known for *Treasure Island* and *A Child's Garden of Verses*

Stevenson's adventure stories, such as *Treasure Island* and *Kidnapped*, made him a popular writer.

Robert Frost (1874–1963)

Born: San Francisco, California

Occupation: Poet, teacher, farmer

Best known for lyric poems and story poems about nature and country life

Frost is considered one of the greatest U.S. poets of the 1900s.

Edna St. Vincent Millay (1892–1950)

Born: Rockland, Maine

Occupation: Poet and playwright

Best known for lyric poems

Millay was the first woman to win the Pulitzer Prize for Poetry, a major honor for U.S. poets.

Maya Angelou (born 1928)

Born: St. Louis, Missouri

Occupation: Writer, poet

Best known for stories about her own life

Angelou has written over a dozen books of poetry.

Maya Angelou is one of the most famous and respected U.S. poets of the early 21st century.

Glossary

alliteration repetition of beginning letters and sounds. Tongue twisters use alliteration.

assonance repetition of vowel sounds within words. The words *lake* and *day* are examples of assonance.

ballad story poem with short stanzas. Many popular songs are ballads.

chant phrase or slogan repeated in rhythm

character figure or mark used in writing some languages in place of letters. Chinese and Japanese writing use characters instead of letters.

epic long poem about the adventures of a hero. Ancient Greek poets wrote epics.

figurative language speech or writing that departs from exact meaning to achieve a special effect or meaning

free verse poetry that does not rhyme. Free verse does not follow strict rules of rhyme or rhythm.

haiku three-line poem that developed in Japan

Hindu relating to Hinduism, the religion of many people in India

laureate person who is deserving or receiving special recognition for achievement—for example, for poetry

limerick five-line nonsense poem made popular by English poet Edward Lear. Limericks are funny.

lyric poem short poem with song-like qualities. Many love poems are lyric poems.

lyrics words to a song

metaphor direct comparison of two unlike things. Poets use metaphors to help readers understand difficult ideas.

narrative poem poem that tells a story or describes a special event. Narrative poems are also called story poems.

nonsense poem silly, funny poem that makes little sense

onomatopoeia words that imitate sounds. Describing the sound of a dog as "woof" is onomatopoeia.

personification giving human traits to animals, objects, or ideas. If you write that "the moon says good night," you are using personification.

recite repeat from memory in front of an audience

rhyme repetition of sounds at the end of words or lines

rhyme scheme pattern of rhyme in a poem. Usually the rhyme scheme remains the same in each stanza of a poem.

rhythm pattern of strong and weak accents in a poem. Like songs, most poems have rhythm.

simile comparison of two unlike things using the words *like* or *as*. When you say someone is as smart as a fox, you are using simile.

stanza division of a poem, usually into sections of two or more lines each

stress beat or emphasis in a melody, rhythm, and so on

syllable unit of spoken language consisting of a single, uninterrupted sound

Find Out More

Books

Donegan, Patricia. *Haiku: Asian Arts and Crafts for Creative Kids*. Boston: Tuttle, 2003.

Driscoll, Michael. *A Child's Introduction to Poetry*. New York: Black Dog & Leventhal, 2003.

Prelutsky, Jack. *Pizza, Pigs, and Poetry: How to Write a Poem*. New York: Greenwillow, 2008.

Suggested books to use for choral reading

Schlitz, Laura Amy. *Good Masters! Sweet Ladies! Voices from a Medieval Village*. Cambridge, Mass.: Candlewick, 2007.

Winters, Kay. *Colonial Voices: Hear Them Speak*. New York: Dutton, 2008.

Winters, Kay. *Voices of Ancient Egypt*. Washington, D.C.: National Geographic, 2003.

Websites

Edward Lear Home Page
www.nonsenselit.org/Lear

Giggle Poetry
www.gigglepoetry.com

Writing with Writers: Poetry
http://teacher.scholastic.com/writewit/poetry

Index